I LVE
CHRISTMAS

First published 2016

Pitkin Publishing
The History Press
The Mill, Brimscombe Port
Stroud, Gloucestershire, GL5 2QG
www.thehistorypress.co.uk

Enquiries and sales: 01453 883300
Email: sales@thehistorypress.co.uk

Text written by Geoff Holder.
The author has asserted their moral rights.

Designed by Chris West.

British Library Cataloguing in Publication Data.
A Catalogue record for this book is available from
the British Library.

Publication in this form © Pitkin Publishing 2016.

ISBN 978-1-84165-740-0

Contents

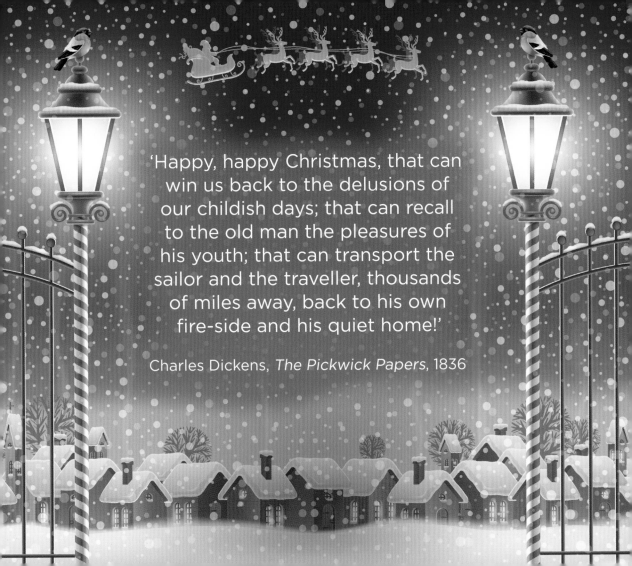

'Happy, happy Christmas, that can win us back to the delusions of our childish days; that can recall to the old man the pleasures of his youth; that can transport the sailor and the traveller, thousands of miles away, back to his own fire-side and his quiet home!'

Charles Dickens, *The Pickwick Papers*, 1836

CHAPTER
ONE

CHRISTMAS
PRESENTS
AND CARDS

1 What do you get the King who has everything? A marmoset. That's what Henry VIII received for Christmas in 1539.

2 Exchanging gifts has been an important part of Midwinter festivals for millennia. During the Roman Empire failing to give presents at this time of year was thought to bring bad luck.

3 We of course associate presents with Christmas Day, but up until the 1860s most people exchanged gifts on New Year's Day.

4 British nobles were required to give cash to the monarch at New Year: by the Tudor era dukes, bishops and earls had to give £20–£30 in gold coins, depending on their rank.

5 An Archbishop, meanwhile, had to hand over a red silk purse holding £40: about £7,000, in modern terms.

6 In exchange, British nobles received metal 'plate' – bowls, tankards, cups, dishes or cutlery – stamped with the royal mark but worth just a fraction of the gold they had handed over. Even worse, they had to tip the royal servants to get anything at all!

7 In 1571 the Earl of Leicester sent Elizabeth I a gold 'armlet', covered with rubies and diamonds, 'having at the closing thearof a clocke': one of the world's first wristwatches.

8 Tudor New Year presents could be unusual too: for example, Sir Edward Horsey sent Queen Elizabeth I a gold toothpick, covered with diamonds and rubies, as her present in 1578.

9 For centuries the Christmases of Kings and Queens were reserved for the exchange of presents between the royal family and their servants. Elizabeth I once received the Tudor equivalent of a Terry's Chocolate Orange from hers: a pie filled with one of the great luxuries of the time, Spanish oranges.

10 Elizabeth I also received a hot-water bottle made of gold: a warming bowl to fill with hot embers from the fire.

11 The term 'pin money' is thought to come from the money Tudor gentlemen put aside to buy their loved one an expensive gold pin at Christmas.

12 Tudors sometimes gave gloves filled with money (called 'glove-money') at Christmastime; Thomas More once got a pair with 40 angels (gold coins) stuffed inside.

13 The workers on Queen Victoria's Osborne estate on the Isle of Wight also received gloves and cloaks at Christmas – not for them, but for their children.

14 Dolls became the must-have present for girls in the 1880s after Queen Victoria bought them for her own children.

15 The present Queen and Prince Philip open their gifts on Christmas Eve – a tradition introduced in the 1840s by Queen Victoria's German husband Prince Albert.

16 In 1662/3 Charles I gave all of his Christmas presents to his mistress, Lady Castlemaine.

17 Christmas Day babies include Humphrey Bogart, who was born on Christmas Day, 1899.

18 Workhouse inmates were often given small presents at Christmas, typically (as at Chard) 'an ounce of tobacco for the men, snuff to the old ladies, and oranges and sweets to the children'.

19 Charlotte Brontë sent Mrs Gaskell a copy of her sister Emily's *Wuthering Heights* as her Christmas present in 1850.

20 In 1940 Winston Churchill sent George VI one of his famous 'siren suits' as a Christmas present.

21 Unusual Christmas presents sold in Harrods' pet department include the alligator bought there for Noël Coward in 1951.

22 What do you get the Queen for Christmas? Kate Middleton made her a jar of chutney. 'I was slightly worried about it,' she told ITV, 'but I noticed the next day that it was on the table … I think it just shows her thoughtfulness, really, and her care in looking after everybody.'

merry xmas

Wishing you a Merry Christmas and a very Happy New Year

23

Wrapping paper was banned during the Second World War: in 1941, the Ministry of Supply ordered that 'no retailer shall provide any paper for the packing or wrapping of goods excepting food stuffs or articles which the shopkeeper has agreed to deliver'.

24 The Christmas card was invented in 1843 by the energetic Sir Henry Cole, who also founded the Victoria & Albert Museum and organised the Great Exhibition. One thousand copies of the first card were printed.

25

The first Christmas card cost one shilling – a day's wages for a labourer. Twenty years later new developments in printing brought the price down so many more people could afford them.

26

John Callcott Horsley's design for the first card offended the Temperance League: it showed children with glasses of wine at the family Christmas dinner.

27 Early Christmas cards were often elaborate affairs – decorated with satin, gilt or sparkly frosting, or luxurious silk tassels. Some even made squeaky noises when you pressed them.

28 A survey of Christmas cards in 1883 showed the most popular illustrations were of people skating on frozen ponds, country houses covered with pristine snow – and snowbound stagecoaches.

29 Prompted by the delays caused by an influx of Christmas cards, the first plea to 'post early for Christmas' was made as early as 1877.

30 Jane Austen's Christmas letter, written to her sister over Christmas Eve and Christmas Day of 1798, was full of jokes about the Christmas ball she'd just been to, and ended with a joking 'I wish you a merry Christmas, but *no* compliments of the season.'

31 In the First World War, for the first time ever, regiments produced their own bespoke cards so the troops could send Christmas greetings to their loved ones from the trenches.

32 Bespoke Christmas cards were also sent to loved ones by the German nationals held in British prisoner-of-war camps, such as the one at Alexandra Palace.

33

Xmas Greetings
7th Division. 1916

Ypres
Neuve. Chapelle
Festubert
Givenchy . Loos
The . Somme

Popular British Christmas postcards sold during the First World War included an image of the Kaiser as a cooked turkey. 'How would you like to "cut in" to this old bird this Xmas?' it asked.

34

In 1914, the teenage Princess Mary published an advert that read: 'I want you now to help me to send a Christmas present from the whole of the nation to every sailor afloat and every soldier at the front ... Could there be anything more likely to hearten them in their struggle than a present received straight from home on Christmas Day?'

35

Princess Mary's fund eventually sent out more than 2.6 million Christmas boxes, despite 45 tons of the brass meant for the boxes going down with the RMS *Lusitania*.

36

Gifts inside Princess Mary's Christmas tin included a monogrammed pencil in the shape of a bullet.

37

Troops in the Second World War paid for deliveries of presents and Christmas trees to their families back home through a scheme run by the YMCA. By 1944 20,000 gifts arrived at British homes this way.

CHAPTER
TWO

CHRISTMAS FOOD AND DRINK

38 An old Italian saying goes: 'Busier than an English oven at Christmas.'

39 Two hundred years ago hardly anyone had turkey for Christmas dinner – the preferred meat was goose, with a joint of beef as a second choice.

40 Turkey arrived as a luxury on the Christmas menu in the 1500s, after the birds were imported from the newly colonised America.

41

However, the popular fashion for turkey only started when Queen Victoria and Prince Albert switched from swan for their Christmas meal in 1851.

42

Upper-class medieval Christmas feasts featured conger eel, sturgeon, heron and swan.
The main meat was a boar's head, brought into the hall to the sound of a traditional carol.

43 One of Henry II's Christmas feasts lasted for nine hours. The menu included luxuries brought back from the Crusades, all washed down with cider and honey.

44 In 1252 Henry III arranged his daughter's wedding for Christmas Day. The feast saw 1,000 knights consume 600 oxen. Cleverly, Henry got an Archbishop to pay for the food.

45 Whole peacocks were sometimes served, complete with the elaborate tail feathers. The meat was roasted with cinnamon and saffron and then sewn back inside the bird's skin.

46 Any uneaten food from royal Christmas feasts was collected in a large silver alms dish and distributed to the poor.

47 In 1770 Sir Henry Grey served his guests a Christmas pie 9ft in diameter and weighing 168lbs. It had to be pushed in on four wheels.

48 Sir Henry's pie contained two woodcocks, two curlews, two rabbits, two ox tongues, four ducks, four partridges, four geese, six pigeons and seven blackbirds, plus 20lbs of butter.

49 In the old days mincemeat sometimes did contain meat: Mrs Beeton, the famous Victorian cook, gave a recipe for mince pies that included minced rump steak.

50

Mince pies used to be known as 'shred pies' – referring to the shredded bits of meat inside them.

51

These days mince pies are circular, but 400 years ago they were oblong, representing the manger of the Nativity, with a pastry baby Jesus on the top.

52

Mince pies were illegal in England for part of the seventeenth century. Even when the law was relaxed, Puritans refused to consume what they saw as a 'Catholic' sweetmeat.

53

The Christmas pudding dates from at least the 1600s, when it was called plum pudding, even though there were no plums in it – 'plum' meant dried currants and raisins.

54 Rather than silver sixpences, in medieval times a bean and a pea were hidden in the pudding. Those who found them were King and Queen respectively for the duration of the feast.

55 Christmas cake – a rich mix of fruits and spices decorated with icing – used to be called Twelfth Night cake. These days it is served anytime in the holidays.

56 Elizabeth I loved chess, so in 1561 her Master Cook, George Webster, made her a Christmas cake in the form of a chessboard.

57 In the West Country, people used to go 'wassailing' at Christmas – sprinkling the trees with cider to make them bear fruit, then getting drunk and dancing round the orchard.

58 Wassail comes from the Anglo-Saxon term *waes hael*, meaning 'be hale' or 'be whole'.

59 A typical wassailing chant went:

'Here's to thee, old apple tree
Hats full, sacks full
Great bushel bags full
Hurrah!'

60 Eggnog has its origins in a medieval drink called posset – hot milk curdled with ale. These days eggnog is a mix of milk, cream, eggs, spices, sugar – and rum or bourbon.

61 Queen Victoria had portions of beef distributed to poor and elderly people at Christmas. The meat was decorated with sprigs of holly taken from the grounds of Windsor Castle.

62 Charles Darwin's crew had a bit too much Christmas cheer aboard the *Beagle* in December 1831: he noted, 'Christmas Day is of great importance to the men: the whole of it has been given up to revelry, at present there is not a sober man in the ship ... the last sentinel came staggering below declaring he would no longer stand on duty, whereupon he is now in irons getting sober as fast as he can.'

63

One group of First World War cooks got so merry they accidentally made their company's Christmas punch with whale oil instead of rum!

64

In many places, officers served Christmas dinner to their men. 'Every officer and every sergeant spent the whole of his time bringing us food and smokes and that,' one London soldier later remembered. 'All smoking away, singing away, food galore ... I shall never forget [it].'

"Cheero!"
XMAS PUDDING XMAS
The 39th DIVISION
TO
BLIGHTY·AND·YOU

Designed by Rifleman Vernon

65

In 1914 Edward VIII – then still a prince – ate his Christmas dinner with his unit, the Grenadier Guards, in France, just a few hundred yards behind the lines.

66

The Christmas menu available to soldiers on the Western Front varied depending on where they were: some lucky soldiers ate rum and roast pheasant, whilst others had to make do with pea soup and bully beef.

Our Seargeant plays Father Xmas for Bill the Ration Scoffer.

67

Rationing during the Second World War hit the traditional Christmas dinner hard – the best most people could manage was rabbit followed by carrot cake made with dried eggs.

68 The Ministry of Food set up a Potato Christmas Fair in the bombed-out John Lewis store on Oxford Street, where a cartoon figure named Potato Pete encouraged people to eat home-grown potatoes.

69 Those whose memories go back to the 1960s will no doubt remember gorging on treats of yesteryear such as Newberry Fruits, crystallised ginger and chocolate liqueurs.

70 On Christmas morning the Queen and Prince Philip attend St Mary Magdalene Church on the Sandringham Estate in Norfolk; then, at 1.15 p.m., they have a Christmas dinner with all the trimmings.

71 Once lunch is over, the staff at Sandringham have the rest of the day off, so the royal couple – and their two-dozen family members in attendance – serve themselves a cold supper.

CHAPTER THREE

CHRISTMAS ENTERTAINMENT

KING WILLIAM the CONQUEROUR

72

William the Conqueror was crowned King of England in Westminster Abbey on Christmas Day in 1066. The celebrations were muted among the defeated Saxons.

73

In the Middle Ages, entertainments – feasting, dancing, putting on 'mummers' plays' and wearing disguises at balls – lasted from Christmas all the way to the climax, Twelfth Night.

From an Antient Limning in the Royal Collection.

KING HENRY VII

74

Money-conscious Henry VII banned card games throughout the year – except at Christmas, when gambling was virtually compulsory for the upper classes.

75

Henry VII's Queen, the usually austere Elizabeth of York, played cards on Boxing Day – and lost. She had to borrow five shillings from the Exchequer to pay her debt.

76

On 3 January 1528, sixteen masked mummers burst into a supper party hosted by Cardinal Wolsey. No one objected, as one of the mummers was the all-dancing, all-partying King, Henry VIII.

77

Elizabeth I loved gambling at Christmas – possibly because the dice were loaded in her favour, so she always won.

78

Several times Elizabeth was forced by fear of the plague to move Christmas celebrations from Greenwich Palace in stinky London to the healthier countryside location of Hampton Court.

79

'If music be the food of love, play on.' William Shakespeare's cross-dressing comedy *Twelfth Night* was first performed for Elizabeth I on Twelfth Night: 6 January 1601.

80

The Puritans banned Christmas plays and similar entertainments in 1642.

81 In medieval times Kings, as well as Oxford Colleges and the Inns of Court, appointed a Christmas 'Lord of Misrule', whose job was to turn the normal world upside down. In the early 1700s this tradition gave way to a new type of Christmas play that eventually birthed a uniquely British tradition – pantomime.

82 The word pantomime literally means 'dumb show'.

83 The first recognisable modern pantomime was *Jack the Giant Killer*, performed at the Theatre Royal in 1773.

84 Modern favourites such as *Aladdin, Mother Goose, Cinderella* and *Babes in the Wood* all date from the eighteenth and very early nineteenth centuries.

85 Charles Dickens first wrote about an idealised Christmas – huge parties, roaring log fires and old traditions – in his 1836 novel *The Pickwick Papers*.

86 The stagecoaches we often see on Christmas cards owe their popularity to Dickens. His nostalgic Christmas stories idealised stagecoaches, which by the 1840s were being replaced by the railways.

87 *A Christmas Carol*, Dickens' ever-popular tale of the miser Scrooge, was published on 19 December 1843. By Christmas Eve it had sold out of its first pressing of 6,000 copies.

88 *A Christmas Carol* is responsible for the association of snow with Christmas. Dickens was nostalgic for his unusually snowy childhood, and incorporated this into the 'scenery' of his story.

89 According to the Met Office, 'widespread snow' at Christmas has only been reported four times in the last fifty-one years in the UK

90 Dickens actually wrote four more Christmas books after *A Christmas Carol* (*The Chimes*, *The Cricket on the Hearth*, *The Battle of Life* and *The Haunted Man and the Ghost's Bargain*), all successful in their own time but largely forgotten now.

91 There have been at least fifty-five versions of *A Christmas Carol* made for film and TV, with around another 150 productions that reference the story in some way.

92 Pop hits from the early 1960s included 'All I Want For Christmas is a Beatle' and 'I'm Gonna Spend My Christmas with a Dalek'.

CHAPTER
FOUR

FATHER
CHRISTMAS

93

We think Father Christmas and Santa Claus are one and the same, but they had two very different origins, one British and the other American. 'Old Father Christmas', also called 'Old Winter' or 'Old Christmas', was a British folk-figure representing winter. If you made him welcome, the season would be kind.

94

Father Christmas originally wore a costume of forest green or deep blue, didn't bring gifts, and dealt exclusively with adults, not children.

95

The Vikings told stories of a cloaked and hooded woman with magical powers who was known as Mother Christmas.

96

Father Christmas, sometimes called Captain Christmas, was often the narrator in the Mummers' plays. Other characters included St George, the Dragon, the Doctor and Beelzebub.

97

One Mummers' play starts:

'In comes I, Father Christmas
Welcome or welcome not
I hope old Father Christmas
Will never be forgot.'

98

In a seventeenth-century play performed for King James I, Father Christmas is described as having a long thin beard and carrying a truncheon.

99

The name 'Santa Claus' comes from St Nicholas, a saint of the fourth century who was renowned for giving money to the poor.

100

Our present-day Santa Claus is fat, jolly and dressed in a red jacket. St Nicholas, in contrast, was always portrayed as thin and serious, and wrapped in a grey cloak.

101

Christmas stockings can be traced to St Nicholas. In the legend, he threw coins down the chimney for three impoverished sisters – and the money landed in their socks drying by the fire.

102

In the early nineteenth century, Dutch immigrants in New York celebrated the festival of Sinterklaas (St Nicolas) on 6 December, when the saint filled children's shoes with presents.

103

English-speaking New Yorkers adapted the custom and shifted it to Christmas, adding new elements. The Dutch Sinterklaas became, in English, Santa Claus.

104

Clement Clarke Moore's 1823 poem *A Visit from St Nicholas* established the modern image: the fat, jolly character with a sack of toys.

105

Moore's poem famously starts:

"Twas the night before Christmas, when all through the house not a creature was stirring. Not even a mouse.'

106

Moore, an American professor and expert in folklore, also created the idea of Santa coming down the chimney, borrowing the image from a Lapland folktale.

107 St Nicholas originally travelled on a flying horse. Moore changed this to a sleigh pulled by flying reindeer, naming them Dasher, Dancer, Prancer, Vixen, Comet, Cupid, Donder and Blitzen.

108 In real life, both male and female reindeer have antlers, but the males shed theirs by midwinter. The antlered reindeer pulling the Christmas sleigh must therefore all be female.

109 Rudolf the Red-Nosed Reindeer only appeared in 1939, the creation of an American advertising agency. His fame was cemented by the hit song of the same name, recorded in 1949.

110 The modern image of Santa Claus also owes a great deal to the Swedish-American artist Haddon Sundblom, who was hired to illustrate an extremely successful Christmas campaign for Coca-Cola in 1931 and used Moore's *A Visit from St Nicholas* as his inspiration.

111

Dating from 1857, 'Jingle Bells', originally called 'One Horse Open Sleigh', was actually written for the American festival of Thanksgiving; the popularity of Santa's reindeer-sleigh shifted the song to Christmas.

112

By the 1870s the images of the British Father Christmas and the American Santa Claus had blended. But which one do British children write to? Mostly Father Christmas.

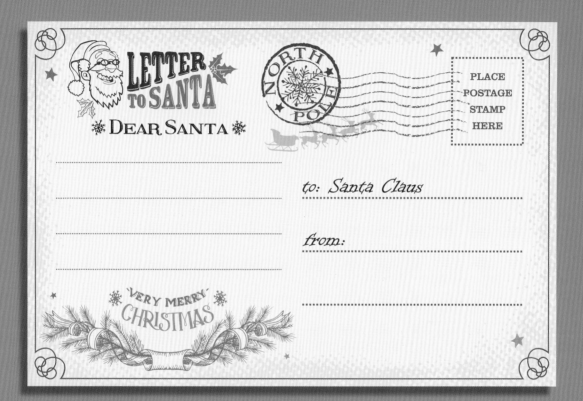

LETTER TO SANTA

✱ DEAR SANTA ✱

NORTH POLE

PLACE
POSTAGE
STAMP
HERE

to: Santa Claus

from:

'VERY MERRY' CHRISTMAS

113 Father Christmas kept up with the times. In 1888 a card showed him taking requests from children – on the new-fangled telephone. A decade later he was delivering gifts by automobile.

114 The first grotto with a Father Christmas in residence was set up in 1888 by the Robert department store in London.

115 Father Christmas and his alter ego Santa Claus get more mail than anyone else in the world. The tradition started centuries ago, with children leaving messages for St Nicholas in the chimney. In 1863 an illustration of Santa reading a child's letter reinvigorated the practice.

116 During the 1920s four Oxford children left letters for Father Christmas by the fireplace. Strangely, they then received illustrated replies from Father Christmas himself. The man who wrote every year from the North Pole and signed himself Father Christmas was actually the children's father J.R.R. Tolkien, author of *The Lord of the Rings*.

117

During the First World War children wrote to Father Christmas not for presents but asking for their fathers, uncles and brothers to return safely from the horror of the trenches.

CHAPTER FIVE

CHRISTMAS DECORATIONS

118 The fir tree at Christmas is a German, not British, creation, with the earliest known example dating from the eighth century.

119 The first decorated Christmas tree in Britain was set up in 1789 by Mrs Papendiek, a servant of the German-born Queen Charlotte, wife of George III. It didn't catch on.

120 In 1800 Queen Charlotte herself had a Christmas tree at Queen's Lodge in Windsor. No one else followed suit, probably because George III was so unpopular.

121 In 1841 Queen Victoria and her German husband, Albert, erected a Christmas tree at Windsor Castle. Victoria wrote that the sight of the tree 'quite affected dear Albert, who turned pale, and had tears in his eyes.'

122

In 1848 the royal
couple were pictured in
The Illustrated London News
beside their Christmas
tree. By 1864 fir trees had
become an indispensable
part of the British Christmas.

123

During Victorian times the tree was crowned with a Union Jack flag, symbol of the British Empire. Over time this changed to a star, an angel or a Christmas fairy.

124

Trees were originally decorated with sweets, bags of cakes and candles – which were of course a fire risk. Wealthy families employed a 'dampener-boy' to extinguish any combusting branches.

125 By the 1880s the popularity of Christmas trees had created a mass-market demand for hanging decorations made of blown glass. Electric fairy lights were invented in America a decade later.

126 In the 1920s there was a fad for artificial Christmas trees made from feathers!

127

In 1941 Winston Churchill attended the lighting of the White House Christmas tree in the company of President Roosevelt, in an America still reeling from the attack on Pearl Harbor.

128

The Christmas tree in Trafalgar Square – the best-known in Britain – has been an annual gift from the city of Oslo since 1947.

129 During the Second World War, the King of Norway escaped the Nazi occupation of his country and headed a resistance government in London. The Trafalgar Square tree commemorates this friendship.

130 The Yule Log is a pagan custom: a tree trunk or branch hauled into the house on Christmas Eve by every able-bodied person (and sometimes oxen as well).

131 The Yule Log was blessed, sprinkled with wine or brandy, then lit with the remains of the previous year's log. It had to last the full twelve days of Christmas. Nobody burns a Yule Log these days, because we don't have the massive fireplaces of yesteryear. Some Christmas cakes now replicate the appearance of the Yule Log.

132

The evergreen leaves of holly represent eternal life, while the red berries symbolise Christ's blood at the resurrection – and the prickly leaves keep evil spirits away. If you pick holly after Christmas Eve, you lay yourself open to attack by evil spirits – or, just as bad, by ill-mannered neighbours!

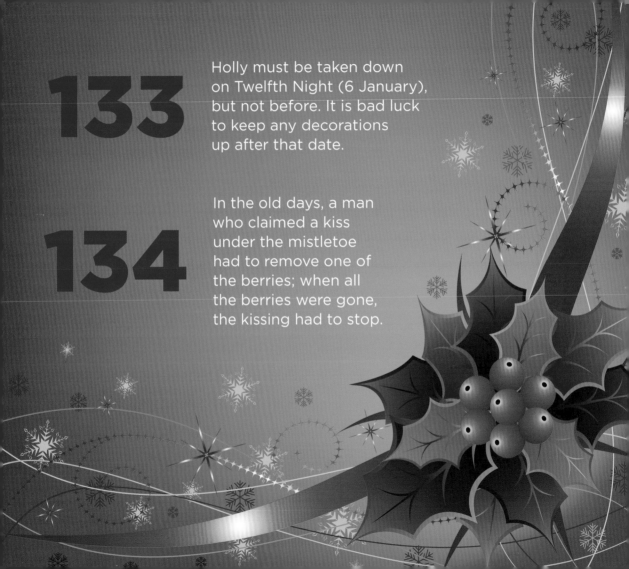

133 Holly must be taken down on Twelfth Night (6 January), but not before. It is bad luck to keep any decorations up after that date.

134 In the old days, a man who claimed a kiss under the mistletoe had to remove one of the berries; when all the berries were gone, the kissing had to stop.

135

In 1940–41 some families decorated their air-raid shelter – reasoning that they spent more time there than in the living room.

136

The seven-stepped candle, now universally popular on Christmas windowsills, is derived from Jewish tradition.

137

The first Christmas crackers
appeared in the 1840s.
The inventor, Londoner
Tom Smith, got the idea from
the way French confectioners
individually wrapped their
sweets with a twist.

138 Mr Smith's first crackers, called bon-bons, contained a motto and a sweet. Over time he replaced the sweets with lucky metal charms such as a black cat.

139 In the 1870s Tom Smith added the tiny explosive that makes the cracker 'crack', changing the name to cosaques, from the noise of the whips used by Cossack horsemen.

140 By the 1880s, however, the word cosaque was replaced by 'cracker'. The motto is now an awful joke, and the metal charm a plastic gift, but the tradition lives on.

141 Tom Smith's descendants hold the royal warrant to supply crackers to the Queen, a privilege they have held since 1964.

142 Those with money to burn can get some truly luxurious crackers from Asprey's, a snip at just £5,000 per box of twelve. They contain suede pouches holding small charms made from pure gold.

CHAPTER

SIX

THE
CHANGING
CHRISTMAS

143

Nobody knows exactly when the first Christian Christmas festival was celebrated, but it was probably about the year AD 320.

144

The ancestry of Christmas lies in two Roman festivals: the birthday of Sol Invictus ('the unconquerable sun') on 25 December, and Saturnalia, a winter period of partying and present-giving.

145

Also in the mix is Yuletide, a twelve-day winter festival celebrated by the pagan tribes of northern Europe, during which there was much feasting, drinking, singing and lighting of bonfires.

146 In pagan Anglo-Saxon times, 25 December was the first day of the New Year.

147 The word Christmas means 'Christ's Mass', from the church service given that day. Other religious festivals with '–mas' names are Candlemas, Martinmas and Lammas.

148 In the 1500s it was illegal to avoid church-going on Christmas Day. The attendance section of the Holy Days and Fasting Days Act (1551) was not actually repealed until 1969.

149 In 1541 the Puritans banned the playing of any sports on Christmas Day. The ban was not enforced, but up to the 1950s thousands of people broke the law every Christmas by attending football matches, the law not being fully repealed until the Betting and Gaming Act of 1960.

150

The Scottish Presbyterian Church banned Christmas in 1583. James I tried to reintroduce the holiday, but the Scots were having none of it.

151

Christmas was illegal in England between 1647 and 1660. MPs attended Parliament on Christmas Day. Town criers walked up and down the streets shouting 'No Christmas! No Christmas!'

152

The absence of Christmas was a serious blow for apprentices and labourers – not because of the ban on partying, but because they wouldn't get their traditional gifts and free food.

153

In 1652 a pro-Christmas mob in Canterbury gave the Mayor, Sheriff, Aldermen and Constables a sound beating. Then the rioters had a game of football in the street.

154

In 1656, a Puritan called Christmas 'the old Heathen's Feasting Day', 'the Profane Man's Ranting Day', 'the Superstitious Man's Idol Day', and 'the Multitude's Idle Day'.

155

In 1657 people attempting to celebrate Christmas in a London church were imprisoned and interrogated by soldiers, and left the service under the barrels of muskets.

POLICE
DEPARTMENT

date
25 DECEMBER   ID 811712

156 For hundreds of years carols were either forbidden or ignored in Christmas church services. Only in 1878 were carols once more officially sung in churches.

157 In 1752 the calendar changed, losing twelve days. Many people refused to alter their habits and continued to observe 'Old Christmas Day' according to the old calendar.

158 By the 1790s Twelfth Night was the main celebration and most people worked on Christmas Day, especially in the rapidly industrialising cities.

159 Some remote communities in Wales and the Scottish islands still celebrate Christmas on 6 January.

160 Christmas was made a bank holiday in 1834. Even then, most people still worked on Christmas morning, being given the afternoon off for dinner with their families.

161 Boxing Day has been a bank holiday since 1871. It was originally known as the Feast of St Stephen or St Stephen's Day.

162 Once upon a time, you looked forward to receiving Christmas cards on Christmas Day – but postal deliveries on 25 December were stopped in 1961.

163 Earlier Christmases had been about the whole community. Christmas in Victorian times became much more centred on the home and the family – especially children.

CHAPTER SEVEN

CHRISTMAS TRADITIONS

164 More people attend church on Christmas Day than at any other time of the year. Midnight Mass on 24/25 December traditionally marks the moment of Christ's birth.

165 Many Midnight Masses were cancelled during the Second World War because it was impossible to black out the churches' large stained-glass windows.

166 Carol singers during the Second World War were ordered not to ring their bells in case people mistook them for air-raid warnings.

167 The radio broadcast of religious carols from King's College Cambridge has been an essential part of Christmas since 1930.

168 As midnight on Christmas Eve approaches, tradition has it that cattle kneel down, and bees hum the 100th Psalm ('Make a joyful noise unto the Lord').

169

Scenes of the Nativity traditionally feature sheep.
As the event took place in the Middle East, it is more
likely the shepherds were watching over herds of goats.

170

Fifteen hundred years ago Advent started on 11 November, and every day for six weeks no one was supposed to eat between sunrise and sunset. These days Advent runs from the fourth Sunday before Christmas to 24 December. Special candles are lit in churches on each of the four Sundays.

171

The Advent Calendar was imported from Germany in the twentieth century. Many Advent Calendars have a window for 25 December, although this is not actually part of Advent.

172 The name 'Boxing Day' comes from the tradition of giving 'boxes' of money or presents to servants and tradesmen on the day after Christmas.

173 Apprentices would visit their master's clients on Boxing Day, shaking an earthenware piggybank for donations. The piggybank was smashed open and the coins shared among the apprentices.

174 Earlier, the 'Christmas Box' was money collected in a box handed round after the church services on Christmas Day. The coins were distributed to the poor the following day.

175 In places, the tradition lives on in Boxing Day tips to dustmen, postal workers and newsgirls and boys. It is also the origin of the Christmas bonus at work.

176

The first royal Christmas broadcast came in 1932, when George V addressed a radio audience of 20 million live from a temporary BBC studio in the King's home, Sandringham House.

177

The text of the first Christmas speech, which began, 'I speak now from my home and from my heart, to you all', was written by Rudyard Kipling, author of *The Jungle Book*.

178

There was no royal broadcast in 1937, as Edward VIII had abdicated three weeks before Christmas.

179

George VI was immortalised in the film *The King's Speech*, in which he overcomes his stutter and inspires the country with his live radio broadcasts. In his first wartime Christmas broadcast, he said, 'We feel in our hearts that we are fighting against wickedness, and this conviction will give us strength from day to day to persevere until victory is assured.'

180

In 1944, six months after D-Day, the King's Christmas message included the words: 'The lamps which the Germans had put out all over Europe were being rekindled and were beginning to shine through the fog of war.'

181

In 1951, for the first time, George VI pre-recorded his Christmas message because he was too ill for a live recording. He died the following year.

182

Those of a certain age may remember gathering around a tiny black-and-white TV screen – possibly the only one in the street – for the Queen's first television Christmas message in 1957.

183

The various Christmas messages have been broadcast from Sandringham House, Buckingham Palace, Windsor Castle, the Royal Albert Hall, the Household Cavalry barracks, Hampton Court Palace – and Auckland, New Zealand.

184

Between 1986 and 1991 the Queen's Christmas message was produced by Sir David Attenborough.

185

It is unlucky to carry anything out of the house on Christmas morning before something else has been brought in.

186

British robins are friendly and bold, and this – with their red breast, most noticeable in winter – makes them an icon of Christmas. Both males and females have the plumage.

187 In 1914 some British and German troops famously crossed over each other's lines and briefly observed Christmas together. Cigarettes, food and wine were exchanged, an impromptu game of football shared, and on one occasion they even joined in the hunt for a rabbit.

188 Tony Allen's fascinating 'World War 1 postcards' website shares a German soldier's account of the famous football game: 'A Scottish soldier appeared with a football ... and a few minutes later a real football match got underway. Us Germans really roared when a gust of wind revealed that the Scots wore no drawers under their kilts.'

189 With the guns silenced for once, a group of Germans sang 'Silent Night' in their trenches, getting a round of applause from the British troops.

190 Both sides then joined in and sang 'Oh Come, All Ye Faithful' together.

191 Neither the British nor the German commanders wanted to see their soldiers 'fraternising' with the enemy, so government reports denied the 'Christmas Truce' of 1914 had ever happened.

192 The events spawned a new official tradition – making sure the troops were well-supplied with food and entertainment at Christmas. That way there was less temptation to have a seasonal truce.

193 Both Tommies in the First World War and British prisoners of war in the Second World War put on pantomimes, with the humour focusing on the essential panto elements – mocking authority and cross-dressing.

194 In medieval times 'carols' were popular songs sung in all seasons. The name comes from the French *carole*, a pagan tradition in which people sang and danced in a circle.

195 Nahum Tate composed 'While Shepherds Watched their Flocks by Night' in 1715, using the 'Christmas Melody' from an opera by the Baroque composer Handel.

196

In 1739 Charles Wesley, a prominent Methodist, adapted a piece of music by the composer Mendelssohn for his carol 'Hark, the Herald Angels Sing'.

197

Many people think Martin Luther wrote 'Away in a Manger'. The actual author was an obscure Dutchman from Pennsylvania who penned the original poem sometime before 1885.

198 'Good King Wenceslas' is a nineteenth-century poem set to music from the sixteenth century and loosely based on the legend of St Wenceslas, who was martyred in Bohemia in the tenth century.

199 'O Little Town of Bethlehem' was composed by Phillips Brooks in Philadelphia in 1868. It was immediately forgotten, and only rediscovered twenty years later.

200 'Silent Night' was written because the church organ had broken down. Joseph Mohr, an Austrian priest, quickly penned the song, which was first performed accompanied by a guitar.

I hope you have enjoyed reading this book.
Happy Christmas!

Picture Credits

All pictures from Shutterstock unless otherwise credited.
Numbers refer to the fact each image is with.